MAILLOL

maillol

by Denys Chevalier

CROWN PUBLISHERS, INC. - NEW YORK

Title page: PORTRAIT OF ARISTIDE MAILLOL, by József
Rippl-Ronay, 1899   Oil, 39½″ × 29½″
Musée National d'Art Moderne, Paris

Translated from the French by:
EILEEN B. HENNESSY

LIBRARY OF CONGRESS CATALOG CARD NUMBER: 78-108088
PRINTED IN ITALY - © 1970 BY UFFICIPRESS, S.A. LUGANO

THE WASHWOMAN, 1896 Bronze, H. 4¾″ Private Collection

C. was tall and thin, a self-taught painter and sculptor, a native of the province of Roussillon, on occasions something of a healer, and a fervent admirer of Maillol. It was 1948, and he was taking me to visit the small farm which had formerly belonged to the sculptor, who had suddenly disappeared in a senseless automobile accident four years before. I had not been fortunate enough to meet Maillol during his lifetime, and until now I had had almost no opportunity to establish direct contact with his work.

In fact, what I knew of him was actually very little: an exhibition at the Petit Palais in Paris, long before the war, to which my father had taken me (I was a schoolboy at the time); his *Homage to Cézanne* and *The Mediterranean* at the Tuileries; the *Memorial to Debussy* at Saint-Germain-en-Laye; the retrospective at the Galerie Charpentier the year before; a few re-

Young Girl Crouching, 1905 Bronze, H. 7″ Private Collection, Paris

productions published in various art magazines; and lastly my visit, only two or three days earlier, to the war memorials at Port-Vendres, Elne, Céret, and Banyuls, as well as to the bronze version of *The Mediterranean* on the patio of the town hall in Perpignan. My youth, to begin with, and then (and especially) the war, with its train of prohibitions, dispersions, and restrictions, had permitted me neither to maintain with the Master the personal relationship which in normal times, had I been older, life would undoubtedly have brought about, nor even to establish the intimate relationship with his art which I would have liked.

This, then, was my first visit to this region of the eastern Pyrenees, to the sunburnt border areas of France and Spain, where the land, the sea, and the mountains are united in such a splendid and distinctive fashion. I had therefore accepted with gratitude C.'s kind offer to show me his native land, of which he was, with good reason, I felt, obviously proud.

This explains why, on this burning afternoon, while man and beast in the valley below us were sleeping, torpid with heat, my cicerone and I were climbing together up this blinding, steep path. I was thinking about the old man who, only a short time previously, at the age of 83, had trod this same road every weekend at certain periods of the year, on his way to Banyuls to see his wife and son. For toward the end of his life, in his longing for that solitude and tranquillity which are indispensable to meditation, the Master had withdrawn with increasing frequency to the isolation of his little farm.

Here, like an anchorite, a kind of hermit, doing his own housework and cooking, he lived in the midst of nature, the vision of which, together with a few carefully chosen books, was his only distraction from his artistic work. Rare were the visitors who ventured to disturb him in this retreat, where his labor was divided among sculpture, painting, drawing, studies and meditation. The one exception, I believe, was a young girl, Dina (later Dina Vierny), his favorite and ultimately his only model, who made the trip from Banyuls twice a day, laden with supplies on the way up and a list of errands on the way down.

And Maillol himself? Although well preserved from the ravages of old age, he required tremendous vitality to climb these slopes, even in mountain espadrilles with rope soles, and lightly dressed in a sailor's middy, his head covered with a large shady beret. What a powerful inner necessity must have driven him, each week, to reconquer once again these peaks, whose immutable serenity seemed to exist only for the purpose of permitting him to satisfy his creative desires!

I pictured him walking without speed, with a supple and sustained effort which kept unnecessary fatigue to a minimum. There was no haste in his stride, which was as rhythmical as that of a craftsman proceeding with simplicity to the place where an unfinished piece of work awaits him that must be successfully completed. He knows that he will arrive, that it is unnecessary to exhibit the slightest impatience, and that the hours he spends walking along this road, in the midst of the splendid natural beauty around him, are not hours wasted in idle distractions. On the contrary, they are a very profitable relaxation and preparation, through the exercise of the body, which leaves the mind completely free to meditate and anticipate the future developments of the creative activity that he is soon to continue within the four walls of his studio.

For everything around him leads him back to his plastic creation: a foothill or a voluptuous ravine that falls like the small of a back, the swelling contour of a solitary cypress reminiscent of the perfect curve of a calf or a thigh.

Seldom, in fact, had a landscape given me such an impression of being not on the scale of man, but rather in his image, or, more precisely, in the image of his forms, proportions excepted. By the imperious animatism which they exuded, these undulations of terrain, hollows, furrows of the vineyards, and dark roofs of thorn bushes in the depressions of the combes could only act, upon a sensitivity as acute and attentive to external signs as that of Maillol, as a series of revelations of anthropomorphic correspondences.

Moreover, this atmosphere with its transparency, in which the light distilled not a heat haze but rather a kind of trembling of the contours of forms in the dry air, was not totally foreign to me. On the contrary, I felt as if I were rediscovering it, as I had known it on the coasts of Sicily, Dalmatia, and Greece, in the islands of the Aegean and Ionian Seas, or, better yet, in certain places in the Peloponnesus and on mainland Greece. The silhouettes of the cypress trees were equally proud, and the olive trees, with their airy and transparent foliage, reminded me of the silvery clusters in the valleys around Delphi. As for the gently curving lines, which dropped like sinuous backs down toward the sea, were they really the last foothills of the Albères mountains, or rather the slopes of Mount Parnassus? The illusion was complete. Nothing was lacking: neither the identical sea close by, nor the dazzling sun, nor the luminous space, which isolated the slightest reliefs with the clarity of a dry-point etching.

We had now reached our destination. Before me a quite spacious building of indeterminate age, constructed of coarse stones and roofed with round tiles, crouched with its sheltered terrace behind a curtain of trees. It was on this terrace, a kind of outdoor workshop (which Dina called her « posing room »), that Maillol drew when the weather permitted – which in this favored climate meant almost always.

It was here, too, that in accordance with his expressed wish, he was to sleep his last sleep thirteen years later when, during a ceremony in 1961 in which official honors were paid him by the French navy, Dina had his coffin transferred here from the cemetery at Banyuls, where it had been temporarily interred. At this moment, however, no distressing thoughts were yet attached to this terrace. (But I doubt, although I have not returned to it since then, that the sculptor's mortal remains have disturbed its peace or changed the profoundly serene nature of the landscape, which is both intimate and imposing.) The Master's last retreat glowed in the sun, on the slope of a small valley at the bottom of which the Roume flowed among fig trees, nettle trees and cork-oaks. It was better situated than the old family farm, which had been inherited by one of his sisters and which is located on the other slope, a short distance in from the road to Banyuls, like the house at Puig del Mas, the ground floor of which had been occupied by the sculptor prior to 1936 while his son, the painter Lucien Maillol, had lived on the first floor.

Seated on a stone, and deafened by the strident voices of the insects, I sat dreaming for a time before the tiers of hills and the view of those plane surfaces which had inspired so many of Maillol's masterpieces. For even before he had finally settled (or, more precisely, resettled) here permanently, in a kind of return to his roots, even while he was still living sometimes at Marly and sometimes at Banyuls, he never ceased to feel, as he had throughout his life, a powerful attraction to these flora and fauna, these mountainous horizons, this southern ambience. For him, as though for an Antaeus, every return to French Catalonia was a genuine necessity, undoubtedly less for the purpose of recovering his strength than of renewing his relationship with that which formed the essence of his psychic potential: the equilibrium of the environment, a certain permanence, and a certain detachment.

He was satisfying, then, not only the desire or the need to refresh his vision before the distinctive morphology of the women of his native province with their round heads, broad hips, and short, powerful legs, but a much more primitive need, namely, that of a way of life and a timeless liberty. For although the artist often utilized the services of various models, his works were never literal or servile copies of them.

The fact is that although formally they are related to the general feminine type of Roussillon, his statues (torsos, nudes, academic studies) are neither replicas nor imitations of a given

THE RIVIERA, around 1898   Oil, H. 37″   Petit Palais, Paris

THE ENCHANTED GARDEN, 1894 Tapestry, H. 75″ × 41″ (detail) Collection Dina Vierny, Paris

10

BATHER, around 1902   Tapestry, H. 39″   Collection Princess Bibesco, Paris

THE SEA, aroud 1895   Oil   Petit Palais, Paris

LEDA, 1900   Bronze, H. 11¹/₂″   Private Collection   ▷

Woman with a Dove, 1905 Terra-cotta, H. 10¼″ Private Collection

YOUNG GIRL SEATED, 1900 Terra-cotta, H. 7″ Collection Dina Vierny, Paris

KNEELING WOMAN, 1899-1900
Bronze, H. 7¾"
Museum of Occidental Art, Tokyo

person or model. The problems of resemblance were always foreign to Maillol's preoccupations; once he had found his path, he remained primarily an authentic creator. In his plastic productions he attained by means of verisimilitude to a higher truth, that of abstract symbols, signs, and archetypes.

His statues, which were thus free interpretations, were created to be sure on the basis of forms that, although certainly plausible, were invented beforehand. The fact that this inventive process was in turn supported, justified, and nourished by preliminary observation, simply indicates very precisely the ultimately quite narrow limits of that observation. Once we have refined upon (but not completely eliminated) the opinion of certain authorities who claim that the sculptor's nudes simply reproduce the particular morphology of the women of his province, only that famous Hellenizing character, which still more numerous authorities believe was the basis of his expression, remains to be discussed.

Maillol's admiration for Greek art and early Greek sculpture (that of Polycletus and Phidias, not that of Praxiteles) is obviously a matter of common knowledge, for he never concealed it. But it would be ill advised to regard it as the determining factor in his experiments and achievements. In addition, the sculptor expressed himself very clearly and on repeated occasions on the subject of his personal tastes within the general framework of Greek art:

> I prefer the still-primitive art of Olympia to that of the Parthenon. It is the most beautiful art that I have seen, that exists in the world. It is an art of synthesis, an art superior to that work of the flesh which we modern artists seek. If I had lived in the sixth century, I would have had the privilege of working with those artists... Phidias is a pinnacle of intelligence, and we shall never again attain to such heights, but I prefer Olympia and the Kore statues.

It is obvious that, since these lines were dictated by a burst of enthusiasm, we should not take too literally either the gentle slap at Rodin (the remark about the flesh) or the both pessimistic and somewhat childish prophecy at the end of the speech. Moreover, this prophecy (which is perhaps less a prophecy than a rather naïve despair) that we shall never again reach « such heights » may indicate the modesty and even humility that, with a sublime pride, constituted several facets of his character, which was simultaneously profoundly paradoxical, economical yet generous, passionate yet detached, exalted and withdrawn, plebeian and aristocratic.

But let us return to the manner in which Maillol viewed archaic Greek sculpure, namely, as a paradigm whose profound signifying reasons it was his role to isolate. It was, after all, the identical manner in which he apprehended the masterpieces of other periods in the history of art — notably, the primitives and the Egyptians. Through the admiration which they inspired in him and the ecstasy into which they plunged him, these works became for him so many stimuli — not models but examples. The lesson which he seems to have retained for his own art concerns the internal architecture characteristic of plastic creation, the lightness of the modeling, the harmony of the forms, and a certain conception of beauty.

However, the observer is obliged to recognize that these esthetic specifications appear in Maillol's earliest works; that is, long before his trip to Greece and his visual acquaintance with the creations of Hellenic civilization in their original setting. It is as if, by virtue of his geographical environment, his atavism, and his inborn culture, he had been from all eternity and without his knowledge a citizen of Athens, a Greek. This considerably limits the importance of the contribution that, according to certain authorities, the land of the gods allegedly made to his work. This is equally true of the concept of beauty, which in its path from the Greeks to Maillol, via the latter's individual temperament, was considerably modified.

NIGHT, 1902-1904   Bronze, 41½″ × 74″   French Government, National Collection

THE SPRING
1896
Wood
16¼″ × 8½″
Collection
Dina Vierny
Paris
▷

◁
YOUNG GIRL
WALKING
Pastel, H. 15″
Private
Collection
Paris

20

BUST OF AUGUSTE RENOIR, 1907 Bronze, H. 11¾″ Private Collection

THE WAVE WOMAN, 1898 Painting, 20¾″ × 17½″ Collection H. de Monfried

THE MEDITERRANEAN, 1902-1903   Bronze, H. 41″
French Government, Tuileries Garden, Paris   National Collection

The Mediterranean, around 1901 (rear view) Marble
Musée Nationale d'Art Moderne, Paris

Two Female Wrestlers, 1900   Terra-cotta, H. 7¾″
Formerly Collection Albert Sarraut. Private Collection, New York

THE COUPLE, 1896 Terra-cotta, H. 9½″
Private Collection, Paris

Woodcut for Ovid's « Art of Love », edited by Philippe Gonin, Paris 1935

For if the morphology of his statues (almost all of which are statues of women) remains serene and fearless, an enemy of that « movement which shifts the lines, » it seeks not so much to attempt to divinize the body as to animalize it, if we may use this term, by the rejection of all express pretext at psychological interpretation. Very strangely, in Maillol's works the highest degree of formal humanism results in a visible intellectual and spiritual dehumanization. The story, rejected, refused, and even forgotten, gives way to a quasi-abstract conception of art.

Not only do these half-length figures, torsos, and nudes express no sentimental idea; in addition, from a certain point of view we could claim that, surpassing that which they appear to be, they become pure volumes, whether oblong, cylindrical, semicircular, or other. This being the case, we should seek and find the undeniable spirituality of this expression on another level, no longer on the level of more or less philosophical, romantic, or literary implications, but on that of pure sculpture, liberated from all anecdotal contingency. This is thus a higher form of spirituality, whose mode of transmission resides exclusively in the study of volumes and their relationships. Above and beyond a type of figuration (whose ambiguous nature I shall later discuss), Maillol thus corresponds to those of his colleagues, both contemporary and later, who solved the same problems by the method of abstraction.

To complete our discussion of the animalization which I mentioned above, we should note that this animalization is especially striking in the faces of his statues, which are impersonal, devoid of the slightest trace of individuality, anonymous, interchangeable. It is, in fact, in the faces or countenances that individualization has as a general rule the greatest tendency to take refuge, obviously much more than in a back or a hip.

Not only do the heads of Maillol's nudes visibly refuse to represent the description of an individual physiognomy. Obstinately, and with great precision, they surround the increasingly exact definition of the imaginary – and imagined – features of an archetype that originates in a vision in which nature is understood globally and as a whole, and not from the restrictive view-point of an anthropomorphism that refers everything back to itself. Moreover, Maillol himself

28

once remarked that a man (or a woman) is no more important, plastically speaking, than any given rock, animal, or bush.

It is undoubtedly in this fashion of considering the universe and the cosmos as a totality, whose elements are all of equal importance and have no hierarchy, that we must find the germ of this kinship between his artistic expression and that of the Far Eastern statuary of certain periods, which some authorities have remarked. Could the sculptor have known of the principles of Zen, which several Western artists had recently tried to apply to their modes of perception? I doubt it. In any event, this kinship (which merited discovery and disclosure) of the quite debatable plan of the formulations should in my opinion replace that of the motivations. The fact is that even in the Greco-Buddhist arts of Gandhara and Khmer, which are seemingly the closest to Maillol, the formulations are considerably removed from him by virtue of their content, which is completely impregnated with spirituality.

The Catalan artist, who is equally far removed from the idealization of the Greeks and the spiritualization of the Khmers, for example, remains a materialist more than a pantheist. There is no trace of metaphysics in his work. Nature, and nature alone, in her innumerable manifestations, remained the sole source from which his sensitivity drew its emotions, just as the plastic art continued to be his sole method of communication with his fellow man. Until the end of his life he was to apply this method to the various disciplines in which he exercised his talent with approximately equal success: book illustration, drawing, painting. Previously, in fact, at a time when sculpture had not yet monopolized the major portion of his creative activities, Maillol had experimented very seriously, with the professional technical conscientiousness which he brought to everything he undertook, with tapestry and ceramics as well as painting.

Maillol, in fact, was a complete artist to whom nothing in the domain of art was foreign. Aided by a supreme skill which undoubtedly resulted from a constantly alert curiosity, every material and every procedure was for him a pretext for expression. Beginning with no special knowledge, he quickly acquired it through intensive work, experimentation, and intuition. Behind

Woodcut for Ovid's « Art of Love », edited by Philippe Gonin, Paris 1935

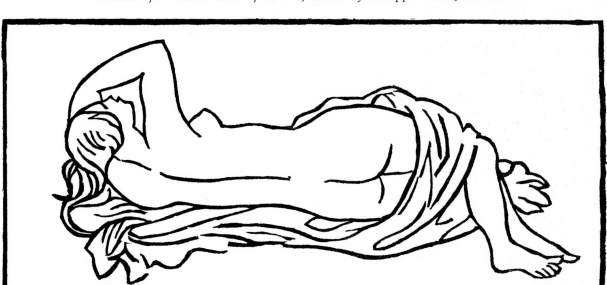

29

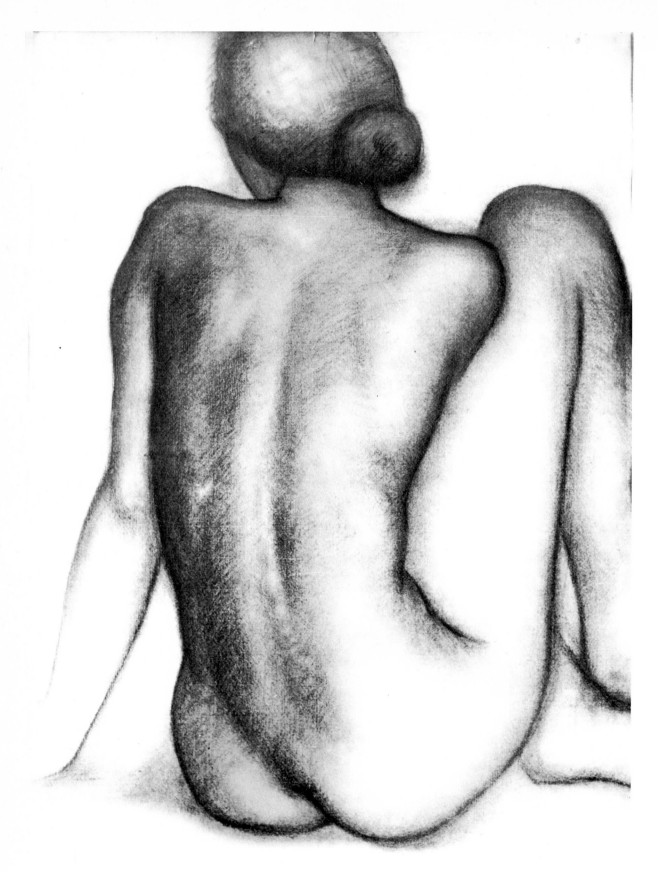

Therese, 1929   Charcoal, 28¾″ × 21½″   Collection Dina Vierny, Paris

the artist there lay concealed a craftsman, or even a jack-of-all-trades, if we consider for example the precarious though ingenious manner in which he constructed his armatures, or used a piece of wood as a tool, or saved a piece of scrap metal with the thought that it could always be useful. His mentality, and the behavior which it produced, bore an incontestably provincial stamp, an earthiness which he had perhaps inherited from his rural middle-class forebears.

For while Maillol came of a family of sailors and landowners, we should not be deceived by these occupations. At Banyuls, his paternal grandfather, the sailor, was by no means an important shipowner: he was the skipper of a modest skiff which engaged in coastal shipping, traveling along the coast from one port to the next. When he had no cargo to transport, he became a sailor, a fisherman, or even on occasion a smuggler.

As for Maillol's father, Raphael, he operated a small fabric business which sometimes obliged him to travel, for the sake of slender profits, to Africa. He also worked a few acres of vineyards that, in view of the small size of the farm, he cultivated himself. The home of Aristide Maillol's parents was much more familiar with want than with wealth or even affluence.

We need not look for any reasons, outside of the frequent traveling done by the head of the family, to account for the fact that while Aristide was still very young, his father entrusted him to his Aunt Lucie, who lived with the old, blind sailor in the latter's home. Moreover, this move eased the pressure on a family budget which was always precariously balanced, and relieved his mother of some additional work and responsibility – for in Raphael's house near the port two young children were already playing, and a third child later came to join them.

Aristide Joseph Bonaventure Maillol, the second of four children (two boys and two girls), was born on December 8, 1861, at Banyuls-sur-Mer, a few miles from the Spanish frontier, in the *département* of Pyrénées-Orientales. He was born in the same decade that saw the birth of Émile Bernard, Bonnard, Sérusier, Roussel, Maurice Denis, Vuillard, Matisse, Kandinsky (who also died in the same year as Maillol), Bourdelle, and Toulouse-Lautrec. Moreover, he maintained close and sustained friendships with several of these artists, who had banded together in the group of the Nabis (with whom Maillol himself was connected).

However, since he did not really begin his career as a sculptor until about the age of 40 (around 1900), he should more correctly be regarded as the contemporary of the following generation, that of Brancusi, Arp, Gonzalez, Gaudier-Brzeska, and Duchamp-Villon. Nevertheless, during the early part of his life (and later as well) he looked not to them but to his predecessors – Puvis de Chavannes, Gauguin, and Renoir. It is, after all, worthy of note that the artists of his age group whose names have come down to posterity include practically no sculptors, with the exception of Bourdelle; Rodin (1840-1917) appears to have completely monopolized position, fame, and plastic importance. It is equally remarkable that when Maillol began to produce, around 1900, his art was as remote from that of the creator of *The Burghers of Calais* as it was from that of his true contemporaries – Gonzales, Duchamp-Villon, and the others. Maillol being still a young sculptor during the early period of Cubism, this movement made no impression upon him. Nor did the first attempts towards the accession of a nonfigurative art.

Having remained faithful to the enthusiasms and friendships of his earlier period, when he was still a painter, his art was formed in a direction parallel to, one could almost say independent of, the sculptural revolutions which marked the beginning of the century. Moreover he was in every way – in his life, his temperament, his esthetics – different from Rodin, as if Maillol's art, in relationship to Rodin's work, had been developed *a contrario*. The man of the South stood in contrast to the man of the North, whose subjective, emotional, and deliberately literary expression he countered with works of objective volumes, denuded of all extra-plastic significance. In reality, Maillol was and remained, at least in his sculpture, a solitary man.

THE CROWNED CHILD, 1893   Oil, 19″ × 15¾″   Private Collection, Paris

His childhood, spent with his ailing grandfather and his very affectionate, although relatively stern, aunt, was already solitary. He rarely played with boys of his own age. After a somewhat erratic schooling, first at the local primary school and then at the Collège de Perpignan, young Aristide returned to Banyuls after his dismissal from the latter establishment. Between the ages of 18 and 20 he remained in Banyuls, practically without any occupation, his sole activity being to try to overcome his aunt's prejudice against his frequently expressed desire to become a painter. Since his high school days, in fact, Maillol had seized every occasion to draw and sometimes even to paint.

Shortly after the death of his father (who had been paralyzed during the last years of his life), and upon the Mayor's recommendation, the Conseil Général of the department granted him a small yearly subsidy of two hundred francs to study drawing at the Perpignan Museum. This was barely sufficient to pay for his anatomy and perspective lessons and his travel expenses. But the instruction given there left him unsatisfied, and after several disagreements with his teacher, he abandoned Perpignan for the second time and returned to Banyuls. Here by chance he came into contact with a student at the Beaux-Arts in Paris. He immediately made his decision: He would go to the capital and learn painting in the famous school in the Rue Bonaparte.

In short, although disappointed by the frustrations which he had until now encountered in his native province, Maillol was by no means discouraged. It is true that he did not know what disillusionments were lying in wait for him. However, his already unshakable determination encouraged him to overcome all obstacles. For the moment, the chief obstacle was his aunt's attitude, her lack of faith both in his vocation and in his chances for success. Ultimately, however, after repeated pleading by her nephew, she gave in and granted permission for his departure for Paris, even giving him a tiny allowance of twenty francs per month – a sum barely sufficient to prevent him from perishing of starvation.

In 1882, at the age of 21, Maillol arrived in Paris. After vain attempts to join Gérôme's studio, he enrolled in a course in clay modeling at the École des Arts Décoratifs. Later, Cabanel accepted him in his studio so that he could prepare for the entrance examination for the painting section of the École des Beaux-Arts. Ultimately he was admitted, but this promotion did not improve his material circumstances any more than it raised the level of his artistic knowledge, which was practically nil, as he well knew. With a strange feeling of humility and eagerness combined, he never ceased to hope that he would meet the teacher who would guide him, like a mentor, through the complex labyrinth of the procedures of artistic creation. Obviously, this hope was not to materialize; and Maillol was to be obliged to seek and find alone, guided only by the Ariadne's thread of his intelligence and sensitivity, the esthetic solutions whose urgency was becoming increasingly evident to him.

Equally serious for him, on a different level, were the deprivations, the malnutrition, the hostility of the climate, the unsanitary conditions of his precarious lodgings, and overwork, which affected his health. Of average stature, but solidly built, and as thin and wiry as a vinestock or shoot (in the Catalan language « maillol » means « young grape vine »), this man, who was to live without illness or infirmity until an advanced age well beyond that of the average life span, was now rejected by the military review board on the grounds of physical unfitness. This diagnosis by the health service, the accuracy of which is above suspicion, demonstrates to what extent the young man's vitality had been altered by the terrible trials he was facing.

Maillol had little to say concerning these trials, but somewhere in his writings he nevertheless confessed:

How did I escape unscathed? I came close to losing my life. Deathly ill as a result of deprivation and lack of care, and knotted with rheumatism, I spent long periods

YOUNG GIRL CROUCHING, 1900 Terra-cotta, H. 6¾″ Private Collection, France

SEATED WOMAN, 1902   Terra-cotta, H. 10¼″   Private Collection

Desire, around 1905 (high relief)
Lead, H. 47¼″ Boymans Museum, Rotterdam

Sorrow, 1921-1923 Bronze
French Government, Tuileries Garden, Paris National Collection ▷

36

THE CYCLIST, 1907 Bronze, H. 38½″ Musée National d'Art Moderne, Paris

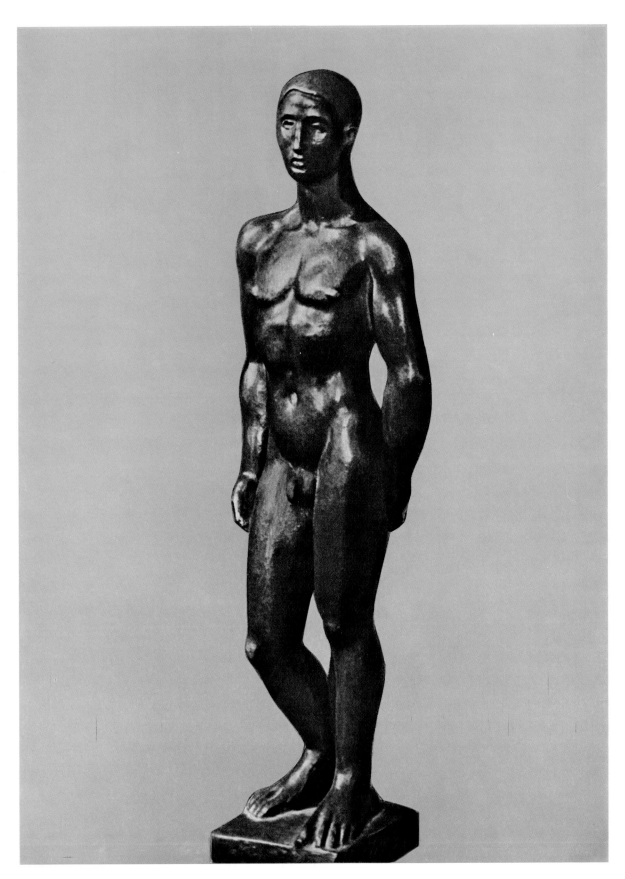

Young Man Standing, 1930 Bronze, H. 12½″ Private Collection

FLORA, 1912 Bronze, H. 64¼″
French Government, Tuileries Garden, Paris National Collection

Ile-de-France, 1925   Bronze, H. 61¼″
French Government, Tuileries Garden, Paris   National Collection

STUDY FOR THE TORSO OF THE MEDITERRANEAN, 1905 Bronze, H. 25″
Collection Heinz Kern, Venezuela

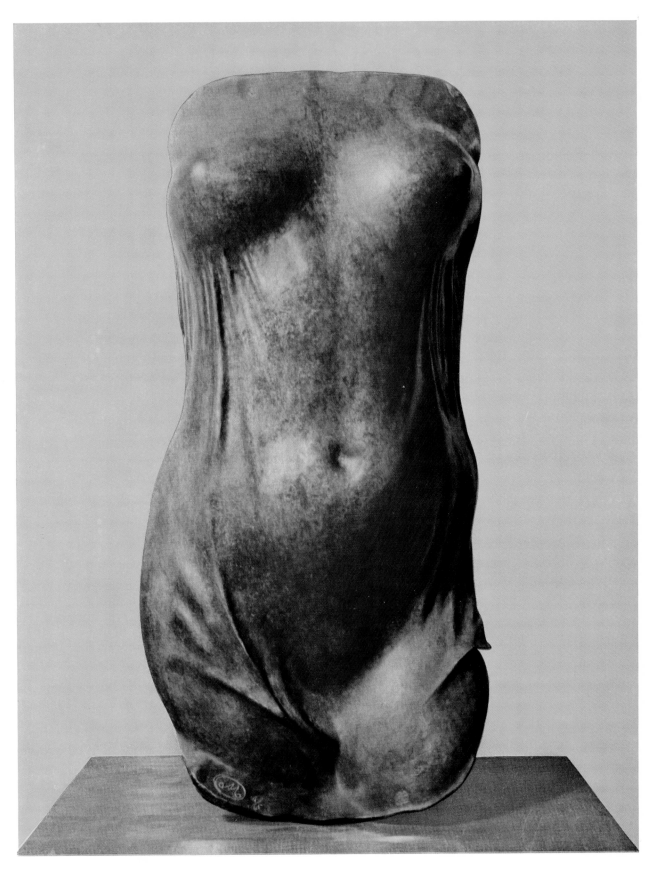

CLOTHED TORSO (relief), 1911 Bronze, H. 24¾″
Private Collection, Paris

MONUMENT TO PAUL CÉZANNE, 1912-1925   Lead, 57" × 87"   French Government, Tuileries Garden, Paris   National Collection

Study for the Monument to Paul Cézanne, 1912 Terra-cotta Private Collection, Paris

Low Relief (detail) for the Soldiers' Monument of Banyuls-sur-Mer, 1930 Plaster original
Collection Dina Vierny, Paris

of time in the hospital, and came out only to fall back into misery. I occasionally thought of putting an end to it by leaping into the Seine.

As moral and material support in his distress, he had only a few young compatriots, artists like himself: the painter Laugé, the sculptor Antoine Bourdelle. He shared a room for a time with the former, and occasionally went to satisfy his hunger in Bourdelle's lodgings. Although he very quickly became convinced of the futility of the official instruction, Maillol remained for about five years at the Beaux-Arts. Most of the students, like the professors, were vulgar undistinguished, and petty. Although Cézanne, Gauguin, and Renoir were at the peak of their activity, their names were barely known, and their works were ignored or derided.

The first beneficent pictorial influence which Maillol experienced was that of Courbet. As a result, he painted numerous canvases in a rather affected spirit, which he eliminated through still-life studies. His early works were frequently painted on coarse sackcloth which he prepared himself, both for the sake of economy and on artistic grounds: he preferred them to the ready-made canvases, which he found too dry and not sufficiently warm.

Each year Maillol returned to spend several months at Banyuls, where he painted, out-of-doors, landscapes full of light and sunshine. The influences of the masters whom he had copied at the Louvre, and later that of Courbet, were now replaced by his admiration for the medieval tapestries preserved in the Cluny Museum, where he had studied them at length around 1892, and by the example of Puvis de Chavannes, at the height of his glory, whose mural and monumental expression had symbolist implications. Maillol had left the Beaux-Arts, and was now teaching in various private academies. At the same time, he was painting several backdrops for Maurice Boucher's little puppet theatre.

Although there were as yet no indications that he was to become a great sculptor, several signs nevertheless seemed, during this period, to predestine his artistic activities to take a monumental direction. Thus, after the Cluny tapestries, several Renaissance tapestries, seen at an exhibition, determined his new orientation. This combination of circumstances, combined with his natural predilection for size and simplicity of style and excellence of materials, triggered a passion hitherto unknown to him, namely, tapestry. It is in truth a strange and little-known phenomenon that long before Lurçat (who is regarded as the reviver of the art of tapestry), around 1893, Maillol was the first to become interested in this discipline, which had somewhat fallen into disuse and which was now seldom practiced except by mediocre craftsmen and decorators without spirit.

Having decided to exploit the mural possibilities of wool, and even while he was creating his cartoons, the artist began by learning, or even reinventing, the techniques of execution. He modestly styled his first achievements in this genre, which he submitted to the Salon de la Nationale des Beaux-Arts, « attempts at tapestry. » Since ready-made wool did not satisfy him, he bought raw wool, which he then had specially spun to order.

At Banyuls he organized a small studio with several young village girls. Now, however, it was the chemical dyes which displeased him. He decided to prepare the dyes himself from plants which he collected from the nearby mountain in the company of one of his young workers, Clotilde Narcisse (whom he married shortly thereafter and by whom he had a son, Lucien). It must be admitted, however, that with the passage of time the color harmonies in most of his tapestries have changed and the colors have faded slightly. However, their principal qualities, namely, the definition of a characteristically mural space, the mastery of style, and the composition of the planes, have remained intact.

Until 1900, that is, for a period of about seven years, Maillol created numerous tapestries,

BATHER KNEELING WITH HEAD DOWN, 1930 Terra-cotta, H. 6½″
Private Collection

utilizing his experience as a painter in their production. The majority of them depict scenes with female figures against pastoral backgrounds. Not only their subjects, but also their style and esthetics, are generally symbolical. Not for nothing had he been for the past few years in close relationship with the best of the artists in the Nabis, group – Maurice Denis, Vuillard, Bonnard, K. X. Roussel, and others.

His woven works were now meeting more and more frequently with a flattering success. They won the approbation of colleagues and collectors as knowledgeable as Gauguin, and later Daniel de Monfreid, the Princess Bibesco, the Queen of Romania, and others. But esteem, however sincere, does not automatically bring affluence in its wake, still less wealth. Thus during one of his frequent returns to Paris he was obliged, with his young wife, to accept Monfreid's generous hospitality.

He appears to have experimented with sculpture for the first time at Banyuls, around 1895. As usual when he was beginning new experiments, his equipment and material were extremely rudimentary: a simple pocket knife and several logs from fruit trees. However, small masterpieces were to be born of what he undoubtedly regarded at the time as no more than relaxation and distraction.

It must be stressed that Maillol immediately began to express himself three-dimensionally not by modeling (as is customary among beginners) but by carving, which apprentice sculptors usually begin later. In deliberate contrast to the usual method, the artist's activity led him to work with clay only after he had discovered in the neighborhood of Banyuls a small deposit of a clay to which he attributed special qualities. Here again, in this very significant detail, it is worth noting how concerned Maillol was with everything that could individualize and singularize his experiments. Unable to be satisfied with solutions that he had not himself discovered, he had to learn everything by personal experience.

On the spiritual plane, this eminently critical attitude, which was characterized by a distrust of procedures and techniques that did not result from personal discovery, was transposed into freedom of behavior. Rarely was an artist so rich in this kind of disdain for ready-made ideas and the most commonly accepted and proclaimed opinions. However, although he constantly verified everything, and more often twice instead of once, Maillol was in no way a skeptic, for his inner need for certainty and the extreme scrupulousness which he brought to everything he undertook were rather a sign of his unshakable confidence in a higher truth.

In any event, just as he had not dared to call his first works in wool « tapestries », timidity prevented him from placing under the heading of « sculpture » the wooden sculptures which he submitted to the Nationale in 1896: he called them *objets d'art*. Nor was he thinking about making a career out of the art of statuary. Tapestry-making occupied practically all of his time, at Banyuls as at Paris, or more precisely in Villeneuve-Saint-Georges, where he settled in 1899.

In contrast to his tapestries, his wooden and terracotta figurines (for which he himself specially constructed a kiln), all designated under the generic title *Bathers*, owe nothing to Gauguin. Throughout his life Maillol professed a deep admiration for Gauguin. His woven works (which often reveal a certain frankly admitted influence of Maurice Denis as well), with their large color areas whose contours are precisely delimited, their style, rich in arabesques, and the unity of their flat construction, testify in convincing fashion to this admiration.

It required an accident, which could have had tragic consequences, to cause Maillol to finally identify as his own the path which destiny appeared to have prepared for him from all eternity. During 1900, as a result of the very close attention required by the use of the weaving loom, the artist felt his eyesight weakening with increasing rapidity. His continual state of anguish during the six months of his temporary blindness brought about his decision to give up his weaving for

ACTION ENCHAINED
(LIBERTY ENCHAINED)
1906
Bronze, H. 84½″
French Government
National
Collection

50

Torso for Action
Enchained
around 1906
Bronze, H. 14½″
Kunsthistorisches
Museum, Basel

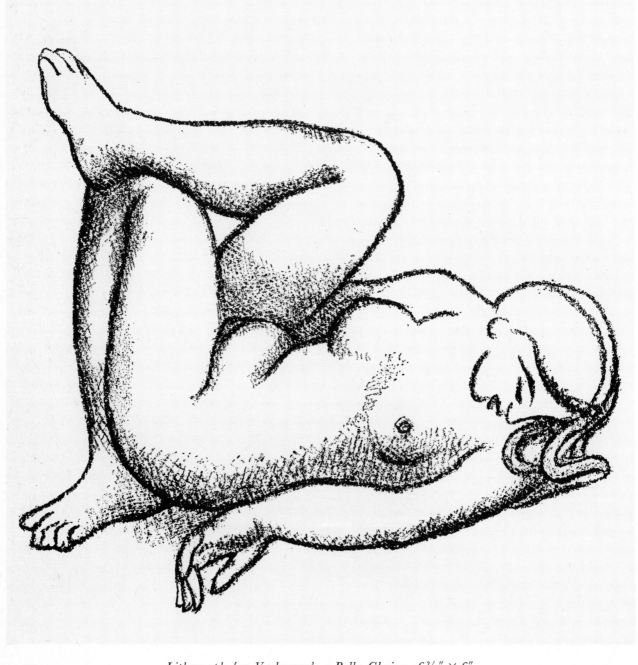

52   *Lithograph for Verhaeren's « Belle Chair », 6¾″ × 6″*
      Editions d'Art Edouard Pelletan, Paris 1931

Squatting Bather, around 1932   Terra-cotta, H. 6¾″   Private Collection

54   Bather with Drapery, 1921 Bronze, H. 69″
French Government, Tuileries Garden, Paris National Collection

good. He did so with some regret, however, for he later confessed that « My tapestry period was the happiest period of my life. »

Sculpture, with its tactile quality, now became his refuge, and seemingly the only artistic activity permitted him. Almost immediately, without hesitations, blind experimentation, or efforts diffused in different directions, he discovered his language. It is true that in addition to his wood sculpture and his terra-cottas, the 39-year-old Maillol already had behind him two or three years of experience with pottery; during one period, he had tried to combine color with volume in small fountains, pieces of pottery, glazed earthenware, and the like.

Moreover, their firing in his small private kiln had, like the dyes of his tapestries, caused him a number of disappointments: objects with surface cracks, objects shattered by the heat and broken in a thousand pieces. But the artist accepted all these accidents philosophically, for in the final analysis few things had the power to affect the equanimity of his humor. One of the reasons, also, for the fragility of his first creations in clay was the unusual method which he used. In these sculptures the volumes were built up by the potter's method, that is, turned around a void and without an armature, rather than being developed in the manner of the modelers; namely, by successive additions of material to a reinforced core. Maillol practiced this method for a long time, and until the end of his life he attached little importance to complicated tools and expensive equipment. Being an ingenious jack-of-all-trades, a minimum of technique, but utilized to the utmost, sufficed him. The tapestry period was now over, but the pottery period was to continue for some years, thanks to a new kiln which he constructed at Villeneuve.

Ambroise Vollard, who had been introduced to Maillol by Vuillard, was now becoming interested in the sculptor. He bought and exhibited several small terra-cottas, and, more importantly, financed his first bronze castings. In 1902 the artist's period of poverty came to an end. His statuettes, which are full of a kind of primitive charm, are reminiscent of Tanagra figurines with their solid yet slender forms. However, a discreet modernism certifies their membership in their age, and his contemporaries, or at least the more sensitive among them – Mirbeau, Berthe Weil, Fagus, and a few others – made no mistake.

A sculptor had been born who was to overthrow the tradition of Rodin and renew the art of sculpture by the introduction of architectural rules. To be sure, the plastic implications of those rules had not yet been fully realized; but already, between the slightly Florentine grace of the pose in *Two Sisters* (1899) and the fleshy robustness of the *Female Wrestlers* (1900), a transition was beginning that, logically, was to encourage the artist to substitute a curvilinear for the rectilinear style. Round, supple rhythms were to replace angular organizations and perfectly perpendicular lines; more serene than severe, however, the forms of an earlier period were still animated by hints of movement.

There followed a succession of works – *Leda, Young Girl with the Dove,* and many other half-length figures, both draped and nude – prior to *The Mediterranean,* the first of his great monumental works, which he began in 1902, interrupted and later resumed, and finally exhibited in 1905. Henceforth nothing was to interrupt the flow of his sculptural creations with the exception of a few short trips (a long trip, in the case of Greece) and the depression into which he was plunged for several months by the death of good Aunt Lucie. Not even his enthusiasm for book illustration and fine library editions (which led him to build, starting from nothing, a manual paper-making plant), and for painting and drawing (which he continued to practice regularly throughout his life) were to deflect him from his course.

Having left Villeneuve-Saint-Georges, Maillol settled in Marly-le-Roi, where he was closer to several of his friends – Vuillard, Maurice Denis, and K. X. Roussel (the two latter, at least, were living in the immediate vicinity of Marly, at Saint-Germain-en-Laye and l'Étang-la-Ville).

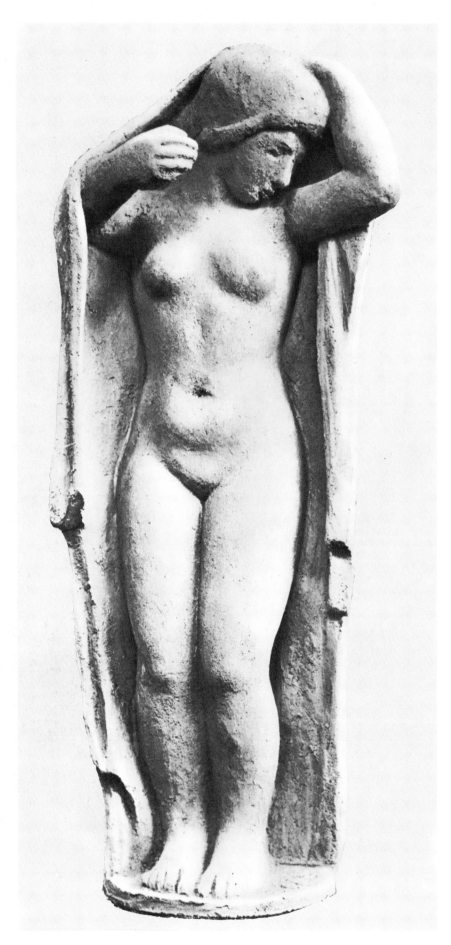

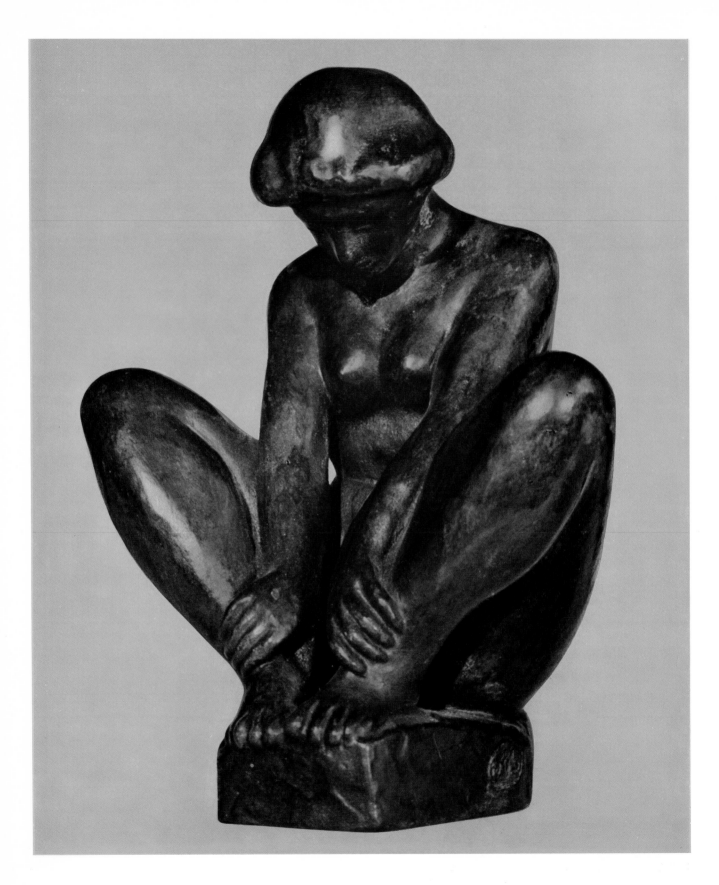

SQUATTING BATHER, 1920   Bronze, H. 6¾″   Private Collection

BUST OF VENUS, 1928   Bronze, H. 21¼″   Private Collection

MEADOW FLOWERS, 1936-1938   Bronze
Musée des Beaux Arts, Poitiers

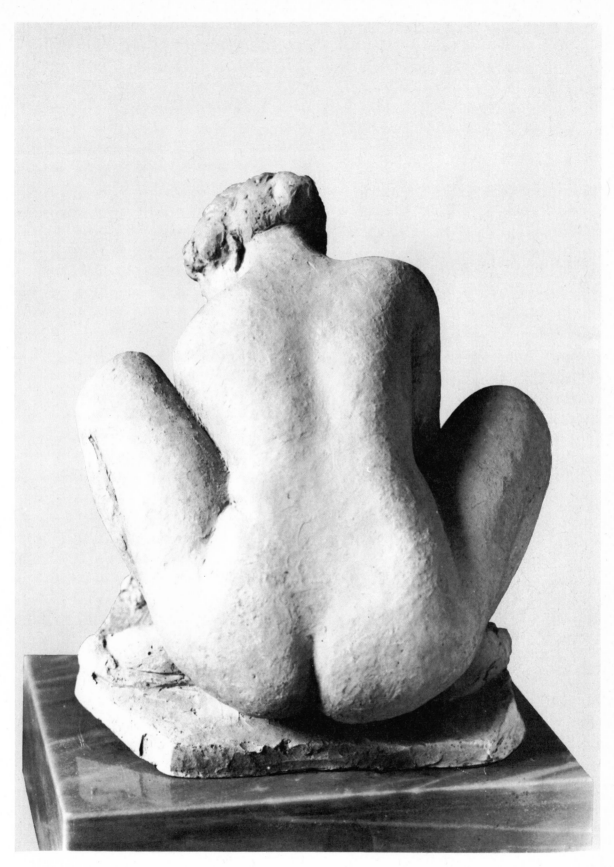

Woman with a Crab (rear view), around 1930   Terra-cotta, H. 6″
Former Collection Bernheim Jeune

The Mountain, 1937 Lead, 64½″ × 72½″
French Government, Tuileries Garden, Paris National Collection

Here he was to live in three houses in succession, the third of which was built according to his own plans. With his style of expression becoming increasingly antagonistic to that of Rodin, he established his position as the successor to the latter's glory. To the same extent that Rodin exacerbated his dynamism in deliberate disequilibriums and expressive projecting areas, revealing the lyrical excitement of his soul, Maillol, repudiating all analytical vision, established the fullness and serenity of the harmonies of synthesis around skillfully calculated central axes or centers of gravity.

The Mediterranean (at first entitled *Statue for a shaded garden,* later *Thought,* and still later *Latin thought*) inaugurates the series of major monuments. It contains the germ of the essence of the artist's message, and achieves in a single effort almost all the objectives which he had now set for himself. It was executed in stone, and cast in several bronze copies from plaster molds made from numerous clay studies.

Throughout his career the sculptor remained faithful to this method of creation, which to be sure was extremely slow but conscientious, and which permitted him to make the innumerable corrections and modifications demanded by his artistic scruples. For direct carving, which presented no particular difficulty for him (as he had clearly demonstrated a few years earlier by carving a *Nymph,* purchased by a German patron), by denying him all prolonged work multiplying to an infinite degree the possibilities of improvements, did not truly correspond to his perfectionist temperament obsessed with the absolute.

Consequently, it is not in the least surprising that the dating of most of his statues almost always includes two dates: that of the original idea or conception, given material form in one or two sketches, and that of the final product, that is, the work regarded by him as completed. In the interval between these two dates, which sometimes spanned a decade, there intervened studies, variations, and more or less profound changes. No improvisation was possible with this method of work, and in Maillol's works spontaneity appears only in the intermediate stages of creation. As the motivating source of that creation, moreover, the artist had from the very beginning regarded spontaneity as an abdication of the will.

Far from being an instantaneous effusion or exaltation, his artistic expression remained, on the contrary, the exclusive fruit of a labor patiently pursued in an orderly manner and with a method which was unvarying in its principles, if not in its results.

With regard to the titles of certain of his works as well, it should also be noted that before being definitely fixed they underwent several changes of wording, as for example in the case of *The Mediterranean, The Bather* (also known as *The Parisian Woman*), and *The Three Nymphs,* which became *The Three Nymphs of the Meadow.* As long as the titles had not been irrevocably assigned, Maillol appears to have been relatively indifferent to the temporary designations of the sculptures in question.

Moreover, these titles were often simply the product of the imagination (not always consonant with the inner feeling of the sculptor) of his poet and writer friends. Nevertheless, trusting in the quality of the affection of those around him, and attentive to their comments, he politely accepted their suggestions and proposals. In his indulgent eyes, this was not a very serious matter.

However – and here is where his good nature ran the risk of working against him – he extended this attitude to the plastic art, or, more precisely, to sculptural composition. The presence of superfluous and slightly anecdotal details in certain of his statues can undoubtedly be explained by the favorable ear which he turned to the words of certain people who were dear to him. Notable examples are the necklace of the *Venus* (1918-1928), the small draped cloth on the back of the *Ile-de-France,* the garland and fruit in the hands of *Flora* (1912) and *Pomona* (1910).

But the sculptor's affability and good nature did not go so far as to obliterate his critical sense, for on several occasions he later removed from one work or another, in new versions, the

After the Bath, Terra-cotta, H. 6¾″ Private Collection, Paris

picturesque elements that he judged to be superfluous. The truth is that nothing in this period was less indicative of his expression than the addition to the plastic art of attributes foreign to it. Far from seeking to add, he was constantly subtracting, saying the maximum number of things with a minimum number of words. This had already been observed in his *Leda* without the swan (definitely the only one of this type) of 1900. In my opinion it remains one of the very rare examples of illusionist sculpture, by the power of suggestion which it brings into play, revealing what does not exist solely by means of the precision of pose and movement.

In 1905 Maillol made the acquaintance of the German Count Kessler, to whom he was introduced by Rodin. This was to prove an event of major importance, both for the development of the sculptor's art and for his life, for if the friendship of the wealthy collector gave his activities an impetus which they would otherwise not have known, it also resulted in disturbances in his life, notably at the time of the First World War, which could have been unfortunate for him.

The wealthy and cultured Count Kessler, who belonged to the cosmopolitan elite of Europe, introduced Maillol into the international milieu of art lovers. He made him known and appreciated especially in the Germanic countries, where the fame of his art soon eclipsed that of all his fellow artists with the possible exception of Rodin. From this period undoubtedly dates, in the mind of Maillol (who compared the welcome given him in his own country with the audience which he found abroad), that kind of naïve Germanism which was later to do him so much harm.

It is true that in 1905, after he had been refused the commission for the memorial to Émile Zola, he had good reason to be angry. In this same year, however, thanks to the intervention of devoted and powerful friends, he was given the commission for the execution of the Auguste Blanqui memorial, known since then by the title *Action Enchained*. Maillol had been a sculptor for hardly five years; moreover, his qualifications for the task of extolling the fiery revolutionary, apart from those conferred on him by his talent, were extremely few.

The sculptor, whose opinions were somewhat conservative, who believed in respect for the traditional political and social values, and who was basically quite indifferent to these problems, barely knew the name of the fighter and martyr for liberty. Those in charge of the undertaking, who revealed a broadmindedness as unquestionable as it was praiseworthy by entrusting to him the task of creating this memorial, were rewarded by a magnificent piece of sculpture, whose torso in particular, with its terrifying eloquence that was somewhat foreign to Maillol's customary style, is in itself a veritable masterpiece, by the violent fury which underlies its volumes, the savage contraction of its movement, and a kind of contained and controlled paroxysm.

It is true that *Action Enchained* was inaugurated only secretly and, so to speak, not inaugurated at all, for the reason that it had not won the approval of the more-than-reticent Municipal Council at Puget-Théniers. However, this is customary in the case of genuinely new and innovative works, and in any case did not merit the arousal of the indignation of a creative artist conscious of being in the right.

Moreover, among French sculptors, Maillol later became the creator of the largest number of memorials (I am not speaking of mass-production manufacturers). Within his lifetime, in fact, his works were erected in Paris, Saint-Germain-en-Laye, Toulouse, Elne, Céret, Banyuls, Port-Vendres, Perpignan, and other places; and after his death he was to share only with Rodin the glory of having his own museum in the heart of Paris, in the Tuileries Gardens. He of all people would appear to have the least right to speak today of an « ungrateful country, » and even then, in 1905, surrounded by devoted friends who were also admirers – painters like Matisse, Bonnard, Renoir; writers like André Gide, Gustave Geoffroy, Henri Barbusse, Octave Mirbeau, Anatole France, and others – he enjoyed incontestable fame and esteem among the elite of the Parisian intellectual and artistic circles.

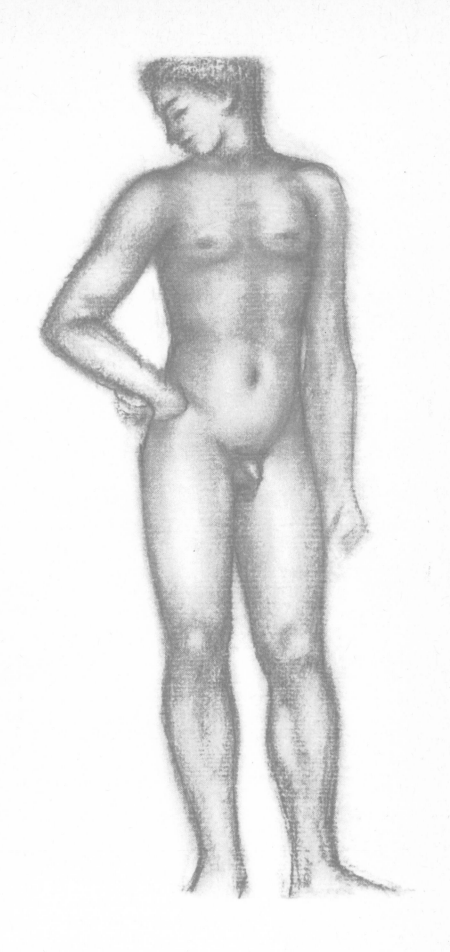

Young Man Standing
Sanguine, H. 11½"
Private Collection

◁

DEBUSSY, 1930
Terra-cotta, H. 11¾"
Private Collection
Stockholm

In reality it is difficult to imagine why he believed he had so much reason to complain about lack of understanding on the part of his compatriots. Of course he was undoubtedly unknown to the common people. But what need had he to be known to them? What pleasure or consolation would he have drawn from a more widely diffused but less well-distributed fame? Why should he have been distressed by the fact that those who were of no importance to him did not acknowledge him?

The esteem of every talented representative France then possessed in the intellectual domain should have more than compensated for the mockery directed at his sculptures by the *Institut*, the representatives of official art, and other partisans of Academicism. It is only good logic, moreover, that if his disdain for the latter was sincere (and nothing permits us to doubt that it was), he should at least have felt that he had been recompensed. Otherwise, by according to these trifling opinions the same importance that he accorded to those of his friends, he was entertaining a strange error of judgment in his mind. But these are mysteries of the human soul, and only a very perceptive psychologist would be able to discriminate between an extreme sensitivity deeply wounded by the mockery of those whom one nevertheless despises and the tremendous pride of the genius conscious of the universality of his worth.

In any event, the widespread admiration aroused by his art both in France and in Europe obliged him to make castings with increasing frequency. He followed his usual method, inventing suitable equipment himself. Just as he had built first a weaving loom and then pottery kilns, so he now (around 1907-1908) set up a foundry for his private use in the rue de Belleville in Paris.

Apart from *Action Enchained,* with its violent lyricism, and another sculpture – *The Young Cyclist,* a longitudinal and angular sculpture, a successor to *The Age of Bronze* – his style developed harmoniously in the direction of an ever-increasing fullness and development in light. For his taut planes, which delimited swollen volumes overflowing with vitality, light was more than a superficial caress or the intermediary indispensable for their optical apprehension. In Maillol's works light becomes a veritable method of plastic expression, a tool.

Being an outdoor sculptor whose artistic expression seemed to be primarily dedicated to grassy spaces and lawns, Maillol organized his masses in an order which maintained their density by preventing them from being nibbled away by space and light. His numerous visits to Versailles, and his elaborate studies of decorative statuary in its parks, familiarized him with the problems posed by the strengthening of the resistance of an opaque body to the dissolving action of daylight.

Reflections on a single subject, combined with the pleasure of experimenting with a material which was new for him but which had already proved its value in the field of outdoor sculpture, led him to create some of his sculptures in lead. Caring little for intermediaries between conception and realization, in most cases he cast them himself.

The rhythm of his success was now becoming increasingly rapid. His patrons could be found throughout the world – in France, in the United States, with Morisov in Moscow, with Oskar Reinhart in Winterthur, and of course there was Count Kessler. It was the latter who, in 1908, during one of the sculptor's rare trips, introduced him to Greece. Maillol's character had nothing of the tourist or explorer anxiously searching for new horizons. The horizons which best suited him (and which were moreover as dissimilar as possible) continued to be the sunbathed Mediterranean coasts and the hills of the Ile-de-France, with their forests laid out like gardens. Throughout his life he remained faithful to these two places, each so very different in atmosphere, moving from one to the other regularly each year.

With the exception of several trips (or rather, excursions) to Spain, and, much later, two or three days in London, the only voyages to which he consented were his trip to Greece with his Maecenas, Kessler, and the writer Hugo von Hofmannsthal; two trips to Germany, in 1928

POMONA, 1910 Bronze, H. 63″
French Government, Tuileries Garden, Paris National Collection

and 1930 respectively; and, lastly, a trip to Italy three years before the Second World War with his colleague Pimienta.

Upon his arrival at Piraeus, Maillol was surprised to discover a geography and a climate which bore a strange resemblance to those of his native land. It is unnecessary to dwell at length upon the expedition of the three friends, the details of which are well known, nor on the enthusiasm into which the sculptor was plunged by the contemplation of the Propylaea, the Kore statues of the Erechtheion, the museum of Olympia, and Delphi with its Aschylian decor; this subject has already been fully discussed elsewhere.

What should be stressed, on the other hand, is the fact that for Maillol this continual and constantly awakened admiration in no way played the role of a hitherto unknown source of inspiration by which his manner, style, and sculptural philosophy were to be regenerated. Rather, it played the role – ultimately an equally important one – of a guarantee, a confirmation, which reinforced his progress along the very personal path which he had carved out for himself. Thus everything permits us to suppose that a visit to ancient Egypt or to certain temples of Buddhist Asia would have brought him the same esthetic satisfactions.

In his studio in Marly he had a mask of Siva, which he valued highly for the pure articulation of its planes, and he envied Rodin a certain Buddha which the Master had purchased. On one occasion, in fact, he confessed, «I would give anything to have a small elephant from India. There is a very great sculpture! The knowledge of planes is common to all the great ages. The Buddhas are very beautiful.»

Thus, despite numerous points of convergence, many things separated him from Greece. How, moreover, would he have been able to forget, in a single experience, Gauguin's teaching? To begin with, antiquity was not fond of women, as Maurice Denis has so correctly emphasized. In Maillol's works, however, the female body, with its ripples, flowing hair, curves and hills, is the very symbol of nature. By means of this body he expresses at one time imposing or familiar landscapes, at another majestic or intimate gardens.

Moreover, we are struck by the great number of titles of his works which call to mind natural phenomena: *The Spring, The Mediterranean, Summer, Night, Air, The Mountain, The Stream,* and so on. Such uniformity could not be the result of chance, and clearly indicates the permanent nature of this outdoor sculptor's inspiration. In his work, the feminine morphology, treated as an inexhaustible store of allegories and symbols, is enriched with polyvalent and ambiguous meanings which evoke both the memory of an action as well as the memory of a given famous person. By means of the symbol, which is something more than it seems to be, the artist's expression surpasses not only resemblance but also representation.

It verges on abstraction, that is, on invention pure and simple, by the organizational priority accorded to the structures. To be sure, any work of art, insofar as its lesson is universally and timelessly intelligible, is abstract, as everyone is aware. What is important is to know in which particular formulative manner this abstraction has been conceived by its creator. The pure plastic sound emitted by the *Christ* of Perpignan, for example, does not have the same origin as that of Manet's *Olympia* or Courbet's *The Wave.* There can be no doubt that the secret of the esthetic absolute revealed in Maillol's art must be sought in the eurythmic disposition of the parts, the disposition responsible for the monumentality of the whole.

This totality, moreover, has its roots less in the body of woman (as I remarked above) than in that of the young girl, the adolescent. Just as Maillol preferred primitive and archaic works of art to those of the so-called ages of high civilization, the chrysalis to the butterfly, and the bud to the flower, he was much more sensitive, under his formal development, to the charm of the young woman (if not the little girl) than to that of the mature woman. That adorable

Bust of Venus, 1920 Bronze, H. 17″ Collection Arthur Stoll Ahrenheim, Basel

awkwardness, that kind of delicate naïvete, that characterize his best statues, are in the last analysis simply the translation of a profound love of youth, which has so far been spared the trials of existence.

For if maturity bears within, if not upon, itself the stigmata of its approaching decline, the germ, embryo, or egg (the same, after all, as that of Brancusi) enfold within their as yet unopened forms, like a promise, all the confidence and hope of world. Maillol, the sculptor of happiness, youth, love, and innocent sensuality, could not hope to discover in some lost paradise, whether Greece or another land, the foundations for that which he was dreaming of creating; they were to be found only in the transparent limpidity of his heart.

He returned to France, enraptured but exhausted, in 1908, and went back to work, completing notably *The Night.* There is nothing to indicate, in this sculpture or in later works, a change, modification, or deviation in his activities which could have been dictated to him by the memory of his Hellenic journey.

After *The Mediterranean, The Night* is the second of his great seated figures whose perimeter is inscribed within a cube. It is superior to *The Mediterranean,* in my opinion, by virtue of the plastic resolution which animates it, and its more highly developed volumetric concentration, which weights it with a kind of secret fervor. It radiates an extraordinary feeling of coiled and confined power. For even in repose there is movement; simply, it is internal and invisible, in short, made abstract.

Two years later, after preliminary conversations with Count Kessler, the head of the art publishing house of Cranach-Press, which published collectors' editions, Maillol allowed himself to be tempted by a new and extrasculptural adventure: book illustration. Actually, it was less a matter of illustration than of complete production and creation, under his complete control, of original works. For, as we have seen, the artist was not concerned with limited, partial responsibilities; he assumed them all and in full. Was there a problem of paper, its quality, weight, texture? No matter, he would make it himself, with the canvas from old boat sails, which he tore up, kneaded, boiled on an old wood stove to reduce it to a pulp, and then spread out to form the product of his industrious ingenuity.

Around 1913, with his friend and Maecenas, he even founded, in the vicinity of Paris, a small plant called Les Papeteries Montval, which continued its activity long after he had ceased to collaborate in the venture and it had been purchased by Montgolfier. Tireless, never discouraged, Maillol worked relentlessly, completely preoccupied with his new passion. Moreover, his paper was a genuine success: sumptuous, heavy, ivorine, with a perfect texture. On this paper he was to illustrate Virgil's *Eclogues,* in Marc Lafargue's translation, with 43 woodcuts and 25 initial letters.

This first book was later followed by numerous others, including three created for the Lausanne publisher Philippe Gonin: Ovid's *Art of Love* (1935), the *Daphnis and Chloe* of Longus (1937), and, posthumously, Virgil's *Georgics* (1950). For Ambroise Vollard Maillol was also to engrave 39 etchings, intended for Ronsard's *Le Livre des Folastries* (1939). After his death, Flammarion published his *Le Concert d'Été,* by J. S. Pons (1946); this was followed in 1948 by Lucian's *Dialogue of the Courtesans,* in a posthumous edition by Creuzevault and Dina Vierny. In addition to these works, which are the most important, Maillol also engraved several plates for a German edition of the *Odyssey* (1930) and for Verhaeren's *Belle Chair* (1931). In 1912 he completed all the plates for the *Eclogues.*

He was predisposed to this work not only by the prints, dry-point etchings, and black-and-white and colored lithographs which he had earlier created, but above all by his remarkable sensitivity as a draftsman. Later, and for other works, he was to utilize on occasion sanguine lithography, which he felt was warmer.

VENUS, 1928   Bronze, H. 29½″
French Government, Tuileries Garden, Paris   National Collection

74

75

THE AIR, 1938   Lead, 54³/₄″ × 100″   French Government, Tuileries Garden, Paris   National Collection

With the exception of the lithographs for the *Dialogue of the Courtesans,* in which the forms of the figures are modeled in chiaroscuro, Maillol expressed himself solely by means of the line, as clearly incised as that of a primitive xylograph. No shading or gradation weakens its linear purity, which is animated solely by contrasts of sharply defined blacks and whites. Only rarely, in a few plates (which are, however, of copper), does he indicate a schematic modeling with the help of coarse cross-hatching.

In order to evaluate these works properly, from the viewpoint of their creator, we must first accept the fact that they have little in common with illustration as it is ordinarily understood. Actually, they neither illustrate, nor even accompany, certain passages of text; more precisely, they form part of the text, within an absolutely original work which foreshadows, long before it became fashionable, the famous book-object so dear to avant-garde enthusiasts of the bibliographic art. In Maillol's words:

> I detest illustrated books. If I am creating them, it is because I feel that line engraving on wood is not illustration; when treated in this way, the drawings are the equivalent of the type. For me, this is typography.

In the same period, which lasted until 1914, he completed *Pomona, Summer, Spring,* and other works, each in several states, and began the *Ile-de-France* and the *Memorial to Cézanne.* The sculptor, who was now 53 years of age, was in full control of his technique and at the height of his production. Visitors came from everywhere, and he was admired throughout the world.

His expression in his figures had now become resolutely synthetic. When seated, they appear to issue from a cube, as I have already noted; when standing, they emerge from a vertical rectangular parallelepiped; when squatting, from a more or less flattened triangular pyramid. Very few in number are the subordinate volumes which extend beyond the ideal frontiers of these invisible frames. Hence the rare character of density in these works, which results not only from the visible compactness of their masses but also from the pressure brought to bear upon them by their illusory outer armature. Thrust outward by the life within them, and blocked in their expansion by this imaginary corset, their planes are located at the exact point in space at which the centripetal and centrifugal forces neutralize each other.

This concentration of forms appears all the more surprising in that it continues to be due solely to the modeling, which as we know can lend itself to the worst excesses. It is true that of this method Maillol retained, not the license which it authorizes, but the hard discipline it requires in order to achieve perfection. Moreover, the artist makes an increasingly frequent compositional use of the possibilities of stability offered him by symmetry. To be sure, this symmetry is never automatic or mechanical; and a margin for fantasy and the unexpected, in the image of life itself, is always left in the regularity of its perpendicular lines. It is nonetheless this symmetry, sensitized, which imprints on the line of its summits, for example, their profoundly melodic aspect.

Maillol's sculpture, which is in truth musical (although devoid of complexity from this point of view) and thus close to the most abstract of the arts, is related to plain song or, more precisely, to unisonal singing, so typical of popular French music. Moreover, the sculptor, whose musical knowledge did not go beyond a frankly average good taste (Bach, Mozart, Beethoven), did not conceal the esteem in which he held the traditional dances and songs of his native province, which like all folk music are crude but expressive, simple, ingenuous, and fresh.

Being unconcerned with the particular, Maillol was interested only in general ideas, and then only in their essence. By means of successive eliminations, he then succeeded in translating their power. Thus the spirit of analysis, originating in the faculties of observation, does not appear at all in his statues; he exercises it at a stage that is prior to their formulation as such. When he models or carves, proceeding in a synthetic (not eclectic) manner, he subtracts, assembles, then condenses and coagulates into new and inseparable entities that which has survived his purifying eliminations.

Thus even the number of sides from which his works can be visually apprehended is, in contrast to Rodin's works, for example, deliberately limited. The minimum, of course, is four, a minimum which Maillol rarely exceeds and which corresponds to this imagined mass of the material which I mentioned earlier. « For me, sculpture is a block, » he admitted. From such a remark, corroborated by others (« I have a weakness for Egyptian sculpture »), we see how deeply the frontality of certain monumental sculptures of early ages had impressed him.

To conclude this discussion of the sections, the sides, and their very special harmonious arrangement in Maillol's art, the unvarying equilibriums as well as the serene and immutable fullness of his works unquestionably flow from the esthetic privation of this expressive method, privileged but ultimately facile, which he imposed upon himself. To the slightly sentimental openness offered by the great diversity of the contours, Maillol preferred the rigorous but supple order of a preliminary lifelike geometry. « I have only a few principal sections, and even these I find too many. I would prefer to have only two sections, like the primitive artists of antiquity. »

Maillol spent the last years of the war in relative tranquillity at Marly, where he was closer to his only son, Lucien, who was drafted in 1916.

However, not until after victory and the return of peace did he have the leisure to resume progress on his major works, the war memorials of Céret and Port-Vendres (inaugurated in 1922 and 1923), and to finish the *Ile-de-France* in 1925, and the *Venus with the Necklace* three years later. With their rhythmical contours and their generous proportions, which exalt the immanence of their presence, the latter resemble columns, with the capital of the head resting on the shaft of the body. The ample development of the forms, whatever the inspiration which guided the sculptor, increases the impression of fullness and serenity which these works diffuse like a wondrous aura about them. Being themselves complete, they in turn fill us with a feeling which is as soothing as a certitude. No directional obliquity, disequilibrium, or instability of planes, which could generate plastic doubts, weaken the exact balance of their relationships.

Minutiosely weighed, these relationships interpenetrate, overlap, and are arranged definitively in what could well constitute the very soul of eternal sculpture. In Maillol's works, despite (or perhaps because of) the generalized nudity of the figures, this sculpture remains astonishingly chaste, including even the strong sexualization of his nudes, which so to speak are never touched by eroticism. Devoid of complexes, and sensually candid, this sexualization demonstrates rather that the artist in no way considers its evidence other than as a knee, a hip, or a neck. For the unique significance which he obviously attaches to it remains plastic in nature. Here, as if at a boundary, his vision begins and ends.

Being a materialist, Maillol never included in his works any ideological, still less mystical, implications. His professed religion was nature, in whose life he saw the symbol of all things. It would perhaps be more proper, moreover, to call him a pagan (as a stoic or, in contrast, a hedonist could be) rather than a materialist. In any event, Maillol apparently remains the only modern artist who never at any time in his career experimented with the subjects of religious iconography.

All his colleagues and friends – from Bonnard to Chagall, from Rodin to Matisse and Léger – were at one time or another attracted by its charms. Not so Maillol. Not because the plasticity of this iconography escaped his attention, but because it comprised a content which was profoundly foreign to him and which would have gravely distorted the very meaning of his work. His personal symbols, the geography of the feminine body, were incompatible with all others.

BATHER WITH RAISED ARMS, 1934 Bronze, H. 64½″
French Government, Tuileries Garden, Paris National Collection

80   CROUCHING WOMAN, 1930 Marble, H. 9¼″ Kunsthalle, Hamburg

It is undoubtedly by virtue of identical considerations that his memorials appear to be marked by such a striking unreality, if not in their execution, then at least in their conception. For the raising of memorials to Blanqui or Cézanne, or of mausoleums to the war dead, by depicting women nude or barely veiled by a draped cloth, was a dangerous enterprise; the sense of homage ran the risk of being weakened. It would unquestionably have been easier and more reassuring to erect a statue of Cézanne himself, for example, with his goatee and his little round hat. Maillol triumphed over these difficulties, and while they lost in subordinate documentary interest, his memorials add to the power and precision of the metaphor, as well as to the sincerity of the feeling, an elegant phrasing which confers upon them their true character as memorial works.

Like pilasters, the legs of most of these standing figures (for example, *Pomona,* among others) accentuate a touch of dissymmetry produced by the slight flexion of a knee, left or right, which continues the barely indicated dislocation of the pelvis. This is the true attitude of inactivity, repose, and vertical inertia; for, as soldiers know, the position of attention implies on the contrary a strain and a tension.

Lithograph: Two Women in the Grass   10" × 14½"

DINA, 1943 Oil, 10¼″ × 14½″ Collection Dina Vierny, Paris

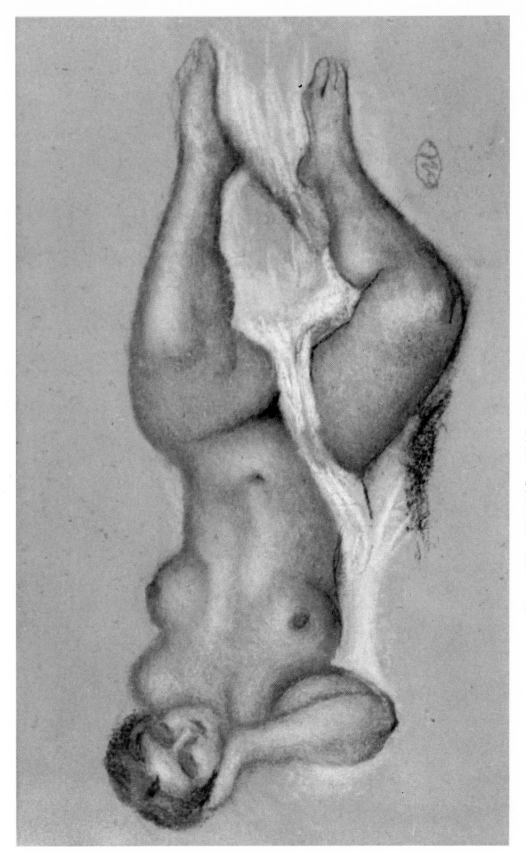

DINA, 1942 Oil, 9¼″ × 14¼″ Collection Dina Vierny, Paris

SEATED BATHER, 1930 Marble, 11″ × 6¼″ Collection Dina Vierny, Paris

STANDING BATHER (rear view), around 1937   Pastel, H. 13″   Private Collection, Paris

*Lithograph for Ovid's
« Art of Love »
edited by Philippe Gonin
Paris 1935*

Nothing of this appears in the arms, whose muscular relaxation is expressed by parallelism. The arms, drawn back in order to set off the bust (as in the *Ile-de-France*), the hands held out in front of the figure (*Pomona*) or symbolically arranged, like a garland, in the center of the composition (the group of the future *Nymphs of the Meadow*), seem to be moved by a single, identical movement; they are not independent, they function in pairs.

I have already spoken of unrealism, but this term should obviously be understood in relation to a naturalistic-literary conception of statuary (from which Maillol was the first to help liberate French sculpture). Being constructed and built, more than sculpted or modeled, his art, or more precisely the manifestations of his art, rise like buildings, with their foundations and subbasements, their various stories and levels, their peaks and ridges.

As the years passed, marked by few but extremely important exhibitions (New York, 1925 and 1933; Berlin, 1928; Basel, 1933; Paris, 1937, at the Petit Palais), Maillol's sculpture developed, refined, and authenticated its architectural essence. Although he was in no way a mathematician or a geometer, Maillol based his activity on squares, triangles, rhombuses, and rectangles, simply because these are the figures which can best be inscribed in space. Regarding the various portions of the anatomy as the plastic accessories of his sculpture, he did not hesitate to take an arm from one of his earlier statues and attach it to the bust of the one on which he was currently working. The same was true for the head and legs.

This freedom of development does not imply a disdain for nature. On the contrary, nature was his only love. Everything he did, he found in nature, but his experiments remained essentially interpretive. Like the perfection of his planes, the smooth and perfect appearance of his surfaces did not aim at imitating the softness or satiny texture of the flesh. The latter, with its palpitations, is rendered differently by the crisp, epidermal modeling of Rodin, for whom the impressionist manner very precisely translates, in the expressive and emotional mode, the perishable and ephemeral nature of the moment. In Maillol's work, on the contrary, in which duration is a primary factor, the unified modeling makes explicit the internal tension of the planes, which has attained its culminating point.

In 1937 Judith Cladel published her *Maillol, sa vie, son œuvre, ses idées*. After Octave Mirbeau and Maurice Denis, who were the first to write texts extolling the sculptor, numerous writers on art – Christian Zervos, Waldemar George, Paul-Sentenac, René Jean, and others – analyzed the particular features of his creative achievement, and defined the major outlines of his decisive contribution to modern art.

Maillol had barely had time to execute several frescoes (at the age of 78 the artist was as enthusiastic as ever for all new methods of expression) when war broke out for the second time – the third war between France and Germany since his birth, for he was ten years old when Bismarck imposed his peace terms on the French Republic with the foundation, at Versailles, of the German Empire. Maillol retired to Banyuls and hved confined in a kind of quasi-retirement, putting the finishing touches to *The Stream* and beginning *Harmony*, his last sculpture, on which he was to work until the end of his life. It is very significant, in my opinion, that this sculpture should have had such a title, a title which is not so much a prophecy as a summary or even a synopsis of his message. It is as if the artist, having had a presentiment of his death, had tried in this sculpture to bequeath to posterity a summary of his work.

During the same period, he returned to painting, which, moreover, had always been for him more than a simple pastime of purely documentary interest. Aided by a distinctive creative instinct, devoid of theories and methods, but guided by the joy of adding a little more beauty to the world, he proved to be as much at ease in landscape as before the study of the female body. Strictly speaking, his painting, which was less closely devoted to the service of the form than, for

THE TWO FRIENDS, 1942   Oil, 8¼" × 13"   Collection Dina Vierny, Paris

example, his drawings, is moreover not a sculptor's painting, for far from being the complement of his principal activity, it constitutes rather the prolongation of that activity into a different sphere.

In contrast to the earlier conflicts, which had not affected him personally (with the exception of the drafting of his son in 1916), this last war, particularly toward its close (and thanks to young Dina Vierny, who was close to his heart and his spirit, and who opened his eyes to political realities whose existence he had not suspected), disconcerted, troubled, and disturbed him. What he was fleeing, in the solitude of his mountains, was not so much the inevitable restrictions of the Occupation as a kind of intellectual night; what he was seeking there was not comfort but isolation and renunciation, as if physical cold was, in short, less unbearable than that of the spirit.

This renunciation, however, was in no way a capitulation, as he proved by working intensively approximately twelve hours a day. It was a pure disdain of the futile and the subordinate – Franciscan, in the tenderness of its love for nature, rather than Pascalian, with the latter's reference to Ecclesiastes' sober words concerning the «vanity of vanities.» It contained, in short, nothing of that desire for abdication and silence, similar to suicide, which is the highest temptation of the proud and to which, abandoning Empire, Tamerlane, Ivan the Terrible, Charles the Fifth of Spain, and Saint-Just, all succumbed. Moreover, it is so obvious that contempt for the goods of this world comes more easily to those who possess all that they want, that I am always surprised to hear them praised for it.

Maillol's last venture, however, sprang from completely different motives. At the height of his fame, having enjoyed every possible success, and now extremely wealthy, the sculptor took refuge in poverty only in order to better preserve the essence of his reasons for living, his true wealth, his art. He was not abandoning, with a nihilistic gesture; on the contrary, he was preserving more closely, he was retaining, by means of a constant communion with nature.

Now completely devoted to the study of nature, he gave final form to that synthesis the idea of which had come to him not by logical deduction, but by observation of the process of growth and development of the flowers, insects, plants, and grass. In this connection, he had long ago remarked, at a time when perhaps he had not yet so clearly expressed it in his works, « I arrived at this idea of synthesis not by reasoning, but by the study of nature, on which I drew directly and by following my sensibility. »

It is clearly the infallibility of his sensibility, which caused him to turn toward beauty and not toward character, that explains the extraordinary plastic quality of the few portraits he painted (notably those of Étienne Terrus and Auguste Renoir). Their draftsmanship is perhaps more nervous than that of his statues, but their formal prospection is carried to equal lengths. For Maillol's portraits, which are at once re-created fragments of nature and works full of grandeur, do not reject expression. They are satisfied to avoid its grimaces, entrusting to immobility and its secret confidences the task of suggesting the meaning to us. Moreover, the immobility of Maillol's works is not that of photographic or other reproductions. It contains *in potentia* all the pulsations of life, with its innumerable possibilities of movement and dynamic virtualities.

Just as in his conversation Maillol spoke more readily of the idea than of the craftsmanship, so he preferred to stress the importance of the form rather than that of the modeling. Extremely light, discreet and luminous, the latter neither attracts nor solicits the beholder's attention by persistent signals or mannerisms; being unstressed, and being above all in the service of form (which itself refers back to the idea, obviously to the plastic idea), it expresses the form in an abstract fashion. This is all the more strange in that the sculptor's formal style, always round, convex, and rich in curves that were more or less soft and full, never ceased to participate very closely in the creations of nature, in which the straight line, that Euclidean invention of man, is

90   Harmony (Torso of Dina), 1943   Plaster Original, H. 48¾″
Collection Dina Vierny, Paris

MASK OF DINA, 1942   Plaster Original, H. 10″
Collection Dina Vierny, Paris

unknown. Perhaps, however, in speaking of his art, we should speak not so much of nature as of life.

At the end of the summer of 1944, while the bells of the Liberation were ringing over Paris and France, Maillol was still working on *Harmony,* for which he had already completed seven states. This sculpture, with its countenance in which for the first time a genuine transcendence of animal nature can clearly be seen, occupies a special place in the Master's work.

More than a summing-up of his earlier work, as I stated above, it represents the beginning of the profound renewal which his art could have known had not destiny reached the end of the allotted span of his days. The tranquil immobility of the volumes is here metamorphosed into peace and serenity, both qualities of the soul. A kind of recollection seems to have presided over the organization of its constitutive masses and their relationships. This organization outstrips and surpasses the classic formalism of all the eminence of a spiritual life that expression has not developed, but liberated. For this is indeed the heart of the matter. In *Harmony* the forms are like an envelope; a splendid plastic, transparent envelope, through which the mechanism of its internal principles can be observed.

On September 15, Maillol was hospitalized in Perpignan, victim of an automobile accident. Several days later he was brought to his house in Banyuls. Here, on September 27, died the artist whose work will continue to be for succeeding generations a major milestone on the royal road of French sculpture.

DENYS CHEVALIER

Study of Nude, around 1902   Sanguine Drawing, H. 9¾"   Private Collection

BIOGRAPHY

1861. Maillol is born on December 8, at Banyuls-sur-Mer. Is immediately turned over to his Aunt Lucie, with whom he spends his childhood and youth.

1874. As a high school student of 13, paints his first picture, a seascape. Decides to become a painter, but does not dare to announce his choice until

1881. When, at the age of 20, he goes to Paris. He is very poor, has no acquaintances or friends. Fails the entrance examination to the Ecole des Beaux-Arts.

1885. After a number of unsuccessful attempts, is finally accepted into Cabanel's studio. However, is disappointed in the teaching at the Beaux-Arts, and leaves almost immediately. Lives alone, in indescribable misery.

1889. Becomes acquainted with Bourdelle.

1893. Goes every day to draw at the Cluny Museum, where he discovers the art of tapestry. That same year, establishes a modest tapestry studio in his aunt's house in Banyuls-sur-Mer; marries one of his employees, and has a son by her. His first tapestry works are a success; at the Salon de la Nationale, Gauguin notices his tapestry, becomes acquainted with and encourages him.

1895. Exhibits a tapestry at the Salon de la Nationale. Exhibits regularly at this Salon until the creation of the Salon d'Automne. Begins to sculpt.

1896. Frequents the « Nabis » group.

1900. His studio at Villeneuve-Saint-Georges becomes a meeting place for the Nabis: Maurice Denis, K. X. Roussel, Thadee Natanson, Pierre Bonnard, Vuillard, the Hungarian painter Rippl-Ronai, the poet Marc Lafargue, Henri Matisse, all of whom remain close throughout their lives. Maillol, now 39 years of age, becomes a sculptor. Vuillard introduces him to Ambroise Vollard.

1902. Exhibits at Vollard's gallery in the rue Laffite. Becomes acquainted with Octave Mirbeau. Rodin praises Maillol's sculpture.

1903. Settles at Marly-le-Roy in order to be close to his friends Maurice Denis and K. X. Roussel. Octave Mirbeau devotes a book to Maillol, and struggles to make him known. Plan for a memorial to Emile Zola is unsuccessful.

1904. Maillol exhibits for the first time at the Salon d'Automne. Meier-Graefe devotes one chapter of his book on modern art to Maillol.

1905. Meets Count Kessler, who becomes his admirer, friend, and patron. « The Mediterranean » is exhibited at the Salon d'Automne. For Gide, « The Mediterranean » is a revelation; it represents a break with the past, with Impressionism and Romanticism. « It is beautiful, it signifies nothing, » he declares in his famous article. « Modern art was to be born of this " Mediterranean." »

1907. Creation of the high relief « Desire » and « The Young Cyclist. » At Renoir's home in Cagnes, sculpts a bust of the painter who, watching Maillol work, is seized with a desire to sculpt.

1908. Trip to Greece with Count Kessler and Hugo von Hofmannsthal. The memorial for Blanqui, «Action enchained, » is completed but not inaugurated at Puget-Théniers; the municipal authorities are horrified, and people are shocked by it.

1909. Exhibits « Night » at the Salon d'Automne.

1910. Executes the first woodcuts for the illustration of Count Kessler's edition of Virgil's *Eclogues*. Exhibits « Pomona » at the Salon. Considerable success in the international art press; first success in the Paris press. The Russian collector Morozoff buys « Pomona » and commissions three other sculptures from the artist, which he calls « The Seasons » (now in the Pushkin Museum in Moscow).

1913. According to Matisse, since 1906 Maillol has been experimenting with the production of a rag paper. He submits his creations to Count Kessler, who establishes a factory for making paper according to Maillol's method. (This paper, known as « Montval, » is still in existence.)

1914. One week before the outbreak of the war, Kessler telegraphs Maillol from Germany, « Maillol, bury your statues, war is here. » This telegram causes Maillol serious difficulties. With the assistance of Clemenceau, he is obliged to prove to the authorities that he is not a spy.

1918. Begins « Venus with the necklace. »

1919. Receives several commissions for memorials, which he executes in stone.

1921. Exhibits « Bather with drapery. » The review of November 6, 1921, declares that « Maillol's statue is arousing the enthusiasm of every visitor. »

1925. The memorial to Paul Cézanne is refused by the city of Aix. The group « Les Amis de Maillol » form a subscription committee for the erection of the memorial. Thanks to President Hériot, the monument is finally bought by the city of Paris, but is not erected.

1928. At the Salon d'Automne, exhibits « Venus with the necklace, » on which he has been working for ten years. Exhibits at the Goupil Gallery in London, and at the Flechtheim Gallery in Berlin.

1929. After a violent campaign in the press, the monument to Paul Cézanne is erected in the Jardin des Tuileries, between two staircases. Due to its private erection, remains completely unknown to the public. The critics protest unsuccessfully.

1930. Participates in L'Art Vivant. Executes memorial to Claude Debussy.

1933. Major exhibition in New York. Retrospective in the Basel Museum. The critics proclaim that « Maillol dominates his epoch. »

1937. Executes « Group of three nymphs. » Maillol exhibition at the Petit Palais.

1938. Receives commission for « The Air, » to be executed in stone and lead; this is to be the memorial to Jean Mermoz. Receives commission for a memorial to his friend Henri Barbusse - « The Stream. »

1941-1942. Works on « Harmony, » which is to be executed in several states. Maillol returns to painting, executes frescoes, draws a great deal. Works with his assistant (who has also been his exclusive model during the past ten years of his life) on the classification and inventory of his work.

1944. In September, Maillol pays a visit to Raoul Dufy at Vernet-les-Bains. Doctor Nicoleau is driving Maillol in his car. There is an accident; Maillol's jaw is injured, and he is no longer able to speak. He writes his last thoughts in a school notebook. He dies at his home in Banyuls on September 27, 1944.

DINA VIERNY

PHOTOGRAPHS

Photographs by the Studio Maywald, Paris, with the exception of: Editions Hyperion Paris (pages 9, 11, 12, 17, 20 22, 23, 36, 39, 45, 56, 64, 66, 67, 85, 86, 92); Max Vaux Paris (pages 50, 76); Flammarion, Paris (page 3); Giraudon, Paris (pages 25, 60, 74); Kunsthistorisches Museum, Basel (page 51); Bernheim Jeune Paris (page 61).

BIBLIOGRAPHY

MIRBEAU Octave: *Aristide Maillol*, Ed. Crès, Paris 1921.

DENIS Maurice: *A. Maillol*, Ed. Crès, Paris 1925.

KUHN Alfred: *Aristide Maillol*, Ed. Seemann, Leipzig 1925.

ZERVOS Christian: *Aristide Maillol*, Ed. L'Art d'Aujour-d'hui, Paris 1925.

LAFARGUE Marc: *Aristide Maillol, Sculpteur et Lithographe,* Ed. Frapier, Paris 1925.

GEORGE Waldemar: *Le Miracle de Maillol*, Ed. Druet, Paris 1927.

LAFARGUE Marc: *Grande Ode au Jardin de Marly et à Aristide Maillol*, Paris 1928.

PAUL-SENTENAC: *Aristide Maillol*, Ed. Peyre, Paris 1936.

RENE-JEAN: *Maillol*, Ed. Braun, Paris 1936.

CLADEL Judith: *Maillol, sa vie, son œuvre et ses idées,* Ed. Grasset, Paris 1937.

DORMOY Marie: *Maillol*, Ed. Arts et Métiers Graphiques, Paris 1937.

REWALD John: *Les Ateliers de Maillol*, Ed. Le Point, Colmar 1938.

REWALD John: *Maillol*, Ed. Hypérion, Paris, London, New York 1939.

APPEL Heinrich: *Das Meisterwerk Maillol*, Bâle 1940.

DENIS Maurice and COLOMBIER Pierre du: *Maillol, Dessins et Pastels,* Ed. Louis Carré, Paris 1942.

PAYRO Julio: *Aristide Maillol*, Ed. Poseidon, Buenos Aires 1942.

REWALD John: *The Woodcuts of Aristide Maillol*, Ed. Pantheon Books, New York 1943.

LAFARGUE M., MIRBEAU O., CAMO P., GIROU J.: *Aspect de Maillol*, Albi 1945.

RITCHIE Andrew C.: *Aristide Maillol 1961-1944,* Ed. Albright Art Gallery, Buffalo 1945.

BOUVIER Marguerite: *Aristide Maillol*, Ed. Marguerat, Lausanne 1945.

ROY Claude: *Maillol vivant*, Ed. Pierre Cailler, Geneva 1947.

CHARBONNEAUX Jean: *Maillol*, Ed. Braun, Paris 1949.

ROMAINS Jules: *Maillol*, Paris 1949.

CAMO Pierre: *Maillol, mon ami*, Ed. du Grand Chêne, Lausanne 1950.

REWALD John: *Aristide Maillol*. Ed. Braun 1950.

TERNOVITZ Boris: *Aristide Maillol*, Ed. Ulrico Hoepli, Milan 1950.

REMSZHARDT G.: *Aristide Maillol, Gefühle der Liebe*, Ed. Feldafing 1954.

KÄSTNER E.: *Aristide Maillol, Hirtenleben*, Ed. Insel, Wiesbaden.

HENRI Frère: *Conversation de Maillol*, Ed. Pierre Cailler, Geneva 1956.

UHDE-BERNAYS Hermann: *Aristide Maillol*, Dresden 1957.

LINNEKAMP Rolf: *Aristide Maillol*, Hamburg 1957.

LINNEKAMP Rolf: *Aristide Maillol und der Goldene Schnitt der Fläche*, Hamburg 1957.

MASIN Jiri: *Aristide Maillol*, Prag 1960.

HACKELSBERGER Berthold: *La Méditerranée*, Stuttgart 1960.

LINNEKAMP Rolf: *Aristide Maillol*, Ed. Bruckman, München 1960.

HOETINK H. R.: *Aristide Maillol, 1963.*

GEORGE Waldemar: *Aristide Maillol et l'âme de la sculpture*, Ed. Ides et Calendes, Neuchâtel 1964.

Etching Illustrating the End of Folastrie V, from Ronsard's « Livret de Folastries »
Editions Ambroise Vollard, Paris

LIST OF ILLUSTRATIONS